The Brotherhood of Religions

By Annie Besant

Copyright © 2021 Lamp of Trismegistus. All rights reserved. No part of this publication may be reproduced or transmitted in any form or by any means, electronic or mechanical, including photocopying, recording, or by any information storage and retrieval system, without permission in writing from Lamp of Trismegistus. Reviewers may quote brief passages.

ISBN: 978-1-63118-563-2

Esoteric Classics

Other Books in this Series and Related Titles

Aurora of the Philosophers by Paracelsus (978-1-63118-507-6)

Clairvoyance and Psychic Abilities by A Besant &c (978-1-63118-403-1)

The Feminine Occult by various authors (978-1-63118-711-7)

Rosicrucian Rules, Secret Signs, Codes and Symbols by various (978-1-63118-488-8)

An Outline of Theosophy by C W Leadbeater (978-1-63118-452-9)

Paracelsus, the Four Elements and Their Spirits by M P Hall (978-1-63118-400-0)

The Stone of the Philosophers by A E Waite (978-1-63118-509-0)

Essays on the Esoteric Tradition of Karma by A Besant &c (978-1-63118-426-0)

The Use of Evil by Annie Besant (978-1-63118-532-8)

The Alchemical Catechism of Paracelsus by Paracelsus (978-1-63118-513-7)

Alchemy in the Nineteenth Century by Helena P Blavatsky (978-1-63118-446-8)

Qabbalistic Teachings and the Tree of Life by M P Hall (978-1-63118-482-6)

The Devil in Love by Jacques Cazotte (978–1–63118–499–4)

Fortune-Telling with Dice by Astra Cielo (978-1-63118-466-6)

History, Analysis and Secret Tradition of the Tarot by Hall &c (978-1-63118-445-1)

Crystal Vision Through Crystal Gazing by Frater Achad (978-1-63118-455-0)

The Golden Verses of Pythagoras: Five Translations (978-1-63118-479-6)

Arcane Formulas or Mental Alchemy by W W Atkinson (978-1-63118-459-8)

The Machinery of the Mind by Dion Fortune (978-1-63118-451-2)

The A E Waite Reader: A Selection of Occult Essays (978-1-63118-515-1)

The Leadbeater Reader: A Selection of Occult Essays (978-1-63118-483-3)

Audio versions are also available on Audible, Amazon and Apple

Other Books in this Series and Related Titles

On the Cave of the Nymphs in the Odyssey by Thomas Taylor (978-1-63118-505-2)

Occult Symbolism of Animals, Insects, Reptiles, Fish & Birds (978-1-63118-420-8)

The Poem of Hashish by A Crowley & C Baudelaire (978-1-63118-484-0)

Brothers & Builders by Joseph Fort Newton (978-1-63118-506-9)

The Kabbalah of Masonry & Related Writings by E Levi &c (978-1-63118-453-6)

A Collection of Fiction and Essays by Occult Writers on Supernatural and Metaphysical Subjects by various (978–1–63118–510–6)

The Sepher Yetzirah and the Qabalah by M P Hall (978-1-63118-481-9)

Kali the Mother by Sister Nivedita (978-1-63118-558-8)

The Hymns of Hermes by G R S Mead (978-1-63118-405-5)

The Secrets of Enoch by Enoch (978-1-63118-449-9)

The Hidden Mysteries of Christianity by Annie Besant (978–1–63118–534–2)

The Sword of Welleran and Other Stories by Lord Dunsany (978-1-63118-501-4)

The Eleusinian Mysteries and Rites by Dudley Wright (978–1–63118–530–4)

Gnosis of the Mind by G. R. S. Mead (978-1-63118-408-6)

The First and Second Gospels of the Infancy of Jesus Christ (978-1-63118-415-4)

The Historic, Mythic and Mystic Christ by Annie Besant (978-1-63118-533-5)

Essays on Ancient Magic by H. P. Blavatsky (978-1-63118-535-9)

Occult Arts by William Q. Judge (978-1-63118-559-5)

The Influence of Pythagoras on Freemasonry and Other Essays (978-1-63118-404-8)

The Path of Light: A Manual of Maha-Yana Buddhism (978-1-63118-471-0)

Tao Te Ching & Commentary by Lao Tzu & C Johnston (978-1-63118-495-6)

Audio versions are also available on Audible, Amazon and Apple

Table of Contents

Introduction...7

The Brotherhood of Religions...9

Symbols...17

Common Doctrines...20

Common Stories...29

Common Ethics...32

INTRODUCTION

The word "esoteric" can be difficult to define. Esotericism in general can be seen less as a system of beliefs and more as a category, which encompasses numerous, different systems of beliefs. It's a bit of juxtaposition, since the word "esoteric" indicates something that few people know about, while the term itself broadly covers numerous philosophies, practices, areas of study and belief systems.

In a greater sense, Esotericism acts as a storehouse for secret knowledge, which is often considered ancient (by *tradition, if not by fact*), passed down from generation to generation, in private. At various times in history, simply possessing the knowledge of some of these subjects, was considered illegal and a jailable offence, if discovered. This usually included such general topics as Alchemy, Pharmacology, Qabalah, Hermeticism, Occultism, Ceremonial Magic, Astrology, Divination, Rosicrucianism and so on. Collectively, these areas of study were often referred to as the esoteric sciences.

Sometimes, the outer garment of a subject isn't esoteric, while what is hidden beneath it, is. As an example, Freemasonry isn't necessarily esoteric by nature (at *least not anymore*), but certain signs, passwords and handshakes given to the candidate during their initiation, are in fact, esoteric, in the sense that they are hidden from the general public.

Today, in the twenty-first century, such topics are readily available at bookstores across the country, and numerous mainsteam publishers offer beginners guides and coffee-table volumes on many of these subjects, intended for mass appeal. Books like *"The Secret"* have turned previously arcane topics into household knowledge. All that being the case, however, it isn't to say that there still aren't buried secrets to uncover, ancient wisdom being ignored and forgotten mysteries to be explored. In fact, it is often that we are only able to further our own studies by standing on the shoulders of these disappearing giants.

Lamp of Trismegistus is doing its part to help preserve humanity's esoteric history by making some of these classics available to those students who are seeking to unearth the knowledge of these ancient colossi.

So, be sure to check other titles from our *Esoteric Classics* series, as well as our *Occult Fiction, Theosophical Classics, Foundations of Freemasonry Series, Supernatural Fiction, Paranormal Research Series, Studies in Buddhism* and our *Christian Apocrypha Series*. You can also download the audio versions of most of these titles from Amazon, Apple or Audible, for learning on the go.

THE BROTHERHOOD OF RELIGIONS

A reader, pausing for a moment on the above title, may very well ejaculate: "Well ! whatever else religions may be, most certainly they are not brotherly." And it is unhappily true that if we look into the religious history of the immediate past, we shall find therein very little brotherhood; rather shall we find religions fighting the one against the other, battling which shall be predominant and crush its rivals to death; religious wars have been the most cruel; religious persecutions have been the most merciless; crusades, inquisitions, horrors of every kind, blot with blood and tears the history of religious struggles; what mockery it seems, amid ensanguined battle-fields and lurid flames of countless stakes, to prate of "the Brotherhood of Religions."

Nor is it even between religion and religion that the continual strife is carried on. Even within the pale of a single religion, sects are formed, which often wage war against each other. Christianity has become a byword among non-Christian nations by the mutual hatreds of the followers of the "Prince of Peace." Roman Catholics and Anglicans, Lutherans and Calvinists, Wesleyans, Baptists, Congregationalists, etc., disturb the peace of the nations with their infuriated controversies. Great Britain and Ireland are now paying the legacy of hatred entailed by the cruel wrongs inflicted on Roman Catholics by the terrible penal code created by a Protestant Parliament; at the present moment (1907) the United Kingdom has been precipitated into a great constitutional struggle by the hatreds of Anglicans and Nonconformists, who cannot even agree on a minimum of common Christian teaching, which may be taught in the national schools to the children of all Christians. France is rent in twain and is in danger of civil war, as a result of the revenge of Freethinkers on the Roman Catholic Church for the wrongs inflicted in the days of its supremacy. In Belgium, political issues are decided by the clerical or anti- clerical majority. Islam has the fierce quarrels of its Shiahs and Sunnis, while both unite in denouncing the infidel Sufi. Even in Hinduism there are now bigoted camps of Vaishnavas and Shaivas, who denounce each other with a narrowness borrowed from missionary examples. Religious controversy has become the type of everything most bitter and most unbrotherly in the struggles of man with man.

It was not always thus. The antagonism between religions is a plant of modern growth, grown out of the seed of an essentially modern claim — the claim of a single religion to be unique and alone inspired. In the elder world there were many religions, and for the most part religion was a national thing, so that the man of one nation had no wish to convert the man of another nation. Each nation had its own religion, as it had its own laws and its own customs, and men were born into and remained in the creed of their fatherland. Hence, if we look back into the history of the elder world, we shall be struck with the rarity of religious wars. Even when the Hebrews invaded Palestine, and murdered the idolatrous dwellers in the land, it was a war of conquest, prompted by ordinary greed, and a war between Jahveh, their particular God, and the Gods of the invaded people; in fact, the general ancient tendency to take into their own religion the Gods of the conquered tribes showed itself many times in their history; this tendency was bitterly denounced by their prophets, not as heresy, but as a national apostasy from their own particular Deity, who had liberated them from Egyptian tyranny and had conquered Palestine for them. We shall further observe that, within a single religion, there were many schools of thought which existed side by side without hatred. Hinduism has its six darshanas — six "points of view" — and, while the philosophers wrangle and debate, and each school defends its own position, there is no lack of brotherly feeling, and all the philosophies are still taught within one tol or pathashal — religious school. Even in one philosophic system, the Vedanta, there are three recognized subdivisions; and Advaita, Vishishtadvaita, and Dvaita — differing on the most fundamental of teachings, the relation between God and the separated spirit — dwell side by side; and fellow-students in the same school learn one, or two, or all of them without attacking each other's orthodoxy. A man may belong to any one of the three, or to none of them, and yet remain a good Hindu, though, as said above, in these modern days, religious sectarianism has become more bitter.

In the mighty Empire of Ancient Rome, all creeds were welcomed, all religions respected, even honored. In the Pantheon — the temple of all Gods — of Rome, the images that symbolized the Gods of every subject nation were to be found, and the Roman citizens showed reverence to them all. And if a new nation came within the circle of the Empire, and that nation adored a form of God other than those forms already worshiped, the images or symbols of the Gods of the new daughter-nation were borne with all honor to the Pantheon of the Motherland, and were reverently enshrined therein. Thus thoroughly was the elder world permeated by the liberal idea that religion was a personal or a national affair, with which none had the right to interfere. God was everywhere; He was in everything; what mattered the form in which He was adored? He was one unseen eternal Being, with many names; what mattered the title by which He was invoked? The watchword of the religious liberty of the elder world rings out in the splendid declaration of Shi Krishna: "However men approach Me, even so do I welcome them, for the path men take from every side is Mine."

The first time that religious persecution stained the annals of Imperial Rome was when young Christianity came into conflict with the State, and the blood of Christians was shed, not as religious sectaries but as political traitors, and as disturbers of the public peace. They claimed supremacy over the older religions, and thus provoked hatreds and tumults; they attacked the religions which had hitherto lived in peace side by side, declaring that they alone were right and all others wrong; they aroused resentment by their aggressive and intolerant attitude, causing disturbances wherever they went. Still more, they gave rise to the most serious suspicions of their loyalty to the State, by refusing to take part in the ordinary ceremony of sprinkling incense, in the fire before the statue of the reigning Emperor, and denounced the practice as idolatrous; Rome saw her sovereignty challenged by the new religion, and while carelessly tolerant of all religions, she was fiercely intolerant of any political insubordination. As rebels, not as heretics, she flung the Christians to the lions, and chased them from her cities into caves and deserts.

It was this claim of Christianity to be the only true religion, which gave birth to religious persecution, first *of* Christianity, then *by* it. For as long as your religion is yours, and mine is mine, and neither claims to impose his religion on the other, no question of persecution can arise. But if I say: "Your conception of God is wrong and mine is right, I only have the truth, and I only can point out the way of salvation, if you do not accept my idea, you will be damned"; then, if l am logical and in the majority, I must be a persecutor, for it is kinder to roast misbelievers here than to allow them to spread their misbelief, and thus damn themselves and others for ever. If I am in a minority, I am likely to be persecuted for men will not readily tolerate the arrogance of their fellow men, who will not allow them to look at the heavens save through their special telescope.

Christianity, from being persecuted, became dominant, and seized the power of the State. The alliance between the State and the Church made religious persecution half political. Heresy in religion became disloyalty; refusal to believe with the Head of the State became treason against that Head; and thus the sad story of Christendom was written, a story which all men who love Religion — be they Christians or non-Christians — must read with shame, with sorrow, almost with despair. And how the "Divinity that shapes our ends" has marked with national ruin the evil results of unbrotherliness in religion! Spain carried on a fierce persecution against the Moors and the Jews; she burned them by thousands, she tortured and mangled them; weary of slaughter she exiled them, and her roads were strewn with corpses during that great exodus, corpses of old men, of women, of nursing mothers, of little children; the tears, the cries of the weak she crushed so pitilessly, became the Avengers who hounded her to ruin, and she sank, from being Mistress of Europe, to the little-regarded Power she is today.

Islam caught from Christianity the deadly disease of persecution, and forsook the wise teachings of Ali to tread the evil path of slaying the infidel. The name of Muhammad the Merciful was used to sharpen the swords of his followers, and in India the doom of the Mogul Empire rang out in the cries of the dying, slaughtered for their faith by Aurangzeb. In India, as in Spain, religious persecution has resulted in political disaster. Thus is the need for brotherliness enforced by the destruction that waits on unbrotherliness. A law of nature is as much proved by the breaking of all that opposes it, as by the enduring of all that is in harmony with it.

The multiplicity of religious beliefs would be an advantage, not an injury, to Religion, if the religions were a brotherhood instead of a battle-field. For each religion has some peculiarity of its own, something to give to the world which the others cannot give. Each religion speaks one letter of the great Name of God, the One without a second, and that Name will only be spoken when every religion sounds out the letter given it to voice, in melodious harmony with the rest. God is so great, so illimitable, that no one brain of man, however great, no one religion, however perfect, can express His infinite perfection. It needs a universe in its totality to mirror Him, nay, countless universes cannot exhaust Him. A star may tell of His Radiance, He the Sun of all, A planet may tell of His Order, revolving in unchanging rhythm. A forest may whisper His Beauty, a mountain His Strength, a river His fertilizing Life, an ocean His changeless Changing; but no object, no grace of form, no splendor of color, nay, not even the heart of man in which He dwells, can show out the manifold perfection of that endless wealth of Being. Only a fragment of His Glory is seen in every object, in every mode of life, and only the totality of all things, past, present and to come, can image out in their endlessness His Infinitude.

And so also a religion can only show forth some aspects of that myriad-faced Existence. What does Hinduism say to the world? It says DHARMA — law, order, harmonious, dutiful growth, the right place of each, right duty, right obedience. What does Zoroastrianism say? It says PURITY — stainlessness of thought, of word, of act. What does Buddhism say? It says WISDOM — Knowledge all-embracing, wedded to perfect Love, love of man, service of humanity, a perfect Compassion, the gathering of the lowest and the weakest into the tender arms of the Lord of Love Himself. What does Christianity say? It says SELF-SACRIFICE, and takes the Cross as its dearest symbol, remembering that wherever one human Spirit crucifies the lower nature and rises to the Supreme, there the Cross shines out. And what does Islam say, youngest of the world's great Faiths? It says SUBMISSION — self-surrender to the one Will that guides the worlds; and sees that Will everywhere, so that it cannot see the little human wills that live only as they blend themselves with It.

We cannot afford to lose any one of these words, summing up the characteristics of each great Faith; so, while recognizing the differences of religions, let us recognize them that we may learn, rather than that we may criticize. Let the Christian teach us what he has to teach, but let him not refuse to learn from his brother of Islam, or his brother of any other creed, for each has something to learn, and something also to teach. And, verily, he best preaches his religion who makes it his motive power in love to God and service to man.

Let us see in detail why we should not quarrel, apart from these general principles. It can be put in a sentence: *Because all the great truths of religion are common property, do not belong exclusively to any one Faith.* That is why nothing vital is gained by changing from one religion to another. You do not need to travel over the whole field of the religions of the world in order to find the water of truth. Dig in the field of your own religion, and go deeper and deeper, till you find the spring of the water of life gushing up, pure and full.

Is the above sentence on the universality of religious truths true in fact, or is it only verbiage? Four special lines of study may be followed in order to prove the fact is thus: common Symbols; common Doctrines; common Stories: common Morals. Each of these headings might be a section of a book entitled *The Brotherhood of Religions,* but in a lecture, or an article, they can only be touched on superficially, with the hope that the listener, or the reader, will turn to the library when the sketch has been placed before him, and make his own the study which has been merely outlined in the sketch.

SYMBOLS

Everywhere in the temples, tombs, and other buildings of dead and living religions, the same symbols are found.

Let us take the Cross. That the cross was used all over the world as a religious symbol long before the time of Jesus, called the Christ, is a matter not for argument but for ordinary reading. Archaeological research has established it for the past, as observation while travelling establishes it for the present. The Etruscan rule was ancient ere infant Rome was born. The Etruscan tombs belonged to a time so remote that, when some of them were opened in our own days, only the first man who entered saw the outline of a corpse, ere it was blown into impalpable dust by the incoming draught of air. But though the man's body was dust, his works remained, and vessels lying at the feet, bowl and platter and vase, spoke of his Faith; on those ancient bits of pottery the cross was traced, telling that the man, whose body had vanished into viewless dust, had died in surety of immortal life, triumphant over death. From Egypt — where it is carven on obelisk, painted on inner chambers where lie mummies in their sarcophagi, frescoed on temple walls — it travelled eastwards through Assyria, Chaldea and India to China. Assyrian tiles, Chaldean pottery, Indian temples, and those of China, wear the cross as treasured symbol of life. Across the Pacific to America travel still; stand in Mexico, where the ancient temples of Maya and Quiche are being unburied by unwearied explorers, and see the Cross, in its Egyptian form, reproduced once more. Travel back across the Atlantic and land in Scandinavia, and from the ancient sagas you hear of the hammer of Thor, the cross once again. Leave the purely religious buildings, and turn to the Masonic Temple, the treasury of ancient symbolism, and there, brought from ancient Egypt, is the Cross upon the Rose — Cross, symbol of life, Rose, symbol of matter and symbol of secrecy as well. Nay, the very symbol of the R. W. M engraved, or worn as jewel, is but the Cross as Svastika refolded on itself, until it makes his badge.

Why is the Cross thus universal? Because it is the sign of Spirit triumphant over matter, molding it, shaping it, forcing it to bear its own impress. It is the symbol of creative power, of the Supreme God sacrificing Himself with the limitations of matter, as in later de-spiritualized days it became the symbol of creative power at the lower, instead of at the higher, pole of being. For the cross as phallic symbol, whereof so much has been made in these later days, is but the cross dragged down to earth from heaven; as, in very truth, the creative power in men, animals and plants, is the reflection, in gross matter, of the Universal Life whereof we all are begotten. Holiest of powers, verily, though degraded to vilest uses. And the Cross meant also, by easy transition, the sure rebirth of life from the tomb or the pyre, the certainty of immortality. Who then shall say, in any exclusive sense: "The Cross is mine?" Mine, as including all. Mine, as excluding none.

And what of the double Triangle, with one apex pointing upwards, and one downwards? This is as universal as the Cross, symbol of the interlacing of Spirit and matter, the fire and water of the elder world. And the five-pointed Star, which is the Jewel in the Lotus, the Self in man. And the seven-pointed Star, and the nine. And the Circle with a Point at the center, or with a Cross within it, or a Cross above or below it. And the Eye, alone or within a Triangle. And the Lotus, or Lily, of Vishnu and of the Virgin Mary. And the whirling Discus, or thunderbolt, of China, of Japan, of India, of Tibet, of Greece, of Rome, of Scandinavia. And the Serpent — of Good and of Evil — and the Dragon, and the Fruit, and the Tree. But time fails me to mention a tithe of the common symbols, common to the earliest antiquity of which traces remain and the latest church built by the most modern architect. And I have said nothing of the symbolism of rites and ceremonies, of the tonsure, and the surplice, and the stole, and the cope; of the upraised hand with two fingers folded and thumb touching, of pope and *pagan* priest; of ceremonial gestures, and symbolical sprinklings — an endless host of details.

There is but One God, one Nature, and one Religion. And symbolism is the common tongue by which all religions tell of their origin from one religion, the WISDOM-RELIGION, the WORLD-RELIGION, ancient yet ever new; and by which also they tell the everlasting truths concerning God and Nature, for the sake of the telling of which they were instituted by the Elder Brothers of Humanity. Symbolism is the common language, and no religion which uses it — and all use it — can claim to be unique.

COMMON DOCTRINES

Let us now pass on to a consideration of the doctrines which are common to the great religions, and we shall find that the fundamental verities on which each religion is built form a common basic structure.

What are these main doctrines? The Unity of God; the Trinity of divine manifestation; the super-physical Hierarchies and their worlds; the Nature of Man; his Evolution; the great Laws. There are others, but in this brief summary I must confine myself to the most important.

1- The Unity of God. Which religion can claim a monopoly of this doctrine? Question the Hindu; he answers: " One only, without; a second." Question the Parsi; he tells of Zarvan Akarana, the Boundless. Question the Hebrew; he replies: "Hear, 0 Israel ! the Lord our God is one Lord". Question the Buddhist; he speaks of One, uncreated, universal, whence creation and particulars come. Question the Christian he answers "There is one God". Question the son of Islam; he cries: "God is God, and there is none other." The great doctors of Islam and the great Vedanta pandits of Hinduism reason on the one universal Existence exactly on the same lines, and these reasonings form one of the bridges between Hinduism and Muslimism over which, we may hope, many a foot will pass in days to come. Religions, in face of these categorical statements from each, cannot quarrel as regards the question of the unity. All each can do is to clothe the one great truth in a different dress, to label it with a different label. But a man remains the same man, though he may change his coat, and a truth remains the same truth, though spoken in different languages. Each religion has its own tongue, and the varieties of tongue mask the identity of belief.

2. The Trinity of Divine Manifestation. To which religion does the teaching of the Trinity exclusively belong? On this point the dead religions of the past reinforce the living religions of the present — as indeed they do all root-truths. The philosophical Hindu says: Sat, Chit, Ananda; the popular voice proclaims: Brahma, Vishnu, Mahadeva. The Buddhist tells of Amitabha, the Boundless Light, Avalokiteshvara and Manjusri; the Parsi, of Ahura-Mazda, Spento and Angro-Mainyush, and Armaiti; the Hebrew, of Kether, Binah and Chockmah; the Christian, of Father, Son and Holy Ghost. The Muslim only, for obvious historical reasons, does not join in the chorus; "He begets not, nor is begotten", says he, alluding to the Christian teaching; and yet out of *Al Quran* shine the attributes, the Mighty, the Merciful, the Wise, so characteristic of the triplicity of Being. This triplicity is best traced by keeping clearly in mind the characteristic marks of each factor — the first, the Fount of Bliss Eternal, of Self-establishment, of Power; the second, the Fount of Consciousness, from whom incarnations proceed; the third, the active Creative Mind which gives existence to the universe.

3. The Superphysical Hierarchies and Their Worlds. Here the difference of tongue, of expression, spoken of above, has given rise to much misconception. In the West, *God* and its equivalents always mean the One, it being further declared by Christianity that each of the Three Persons of the Trinity is God, though in their totality forming one God, not three; there is a unity of nature with a diversity of characteristics. But this word God is never applied in the West to the huge superphysical Hierarchies, who crowd the upper rungs of the ladder of Being. These are Archangels, Angels, Cherubim, Seraphim, Powers, revered, invoked, often worshiped, but recognized as the ministers, the agents, of the Supreme. These beings are recognized by the Parsi as the Ameshaspentas and their hosts; by the Hebrew and the Muslim as Angels; Hindus and

Buddhists call them Devas — literally Shining Ones, a most appropriate descriptive epithet. Unfortunately, Westerners have translated the word Deva as God, and hence we have the thirty-three millions of Gods, about whom ignorant people make fun. The word Brahman is the true equivalent of the English word God, and Deva is Angel. Every reader of English literature knows that John Bunyan, in his *Pilgrim's Progress,* uses this very term, the Shining Ones, to designate the Angels; and it is the natural word for any seer to use, who has seen them flashing through the empyrean on their missions of administration, of succour, of deliverance. The Deva, to the Hindu and Buddhist, is exactly the same as the Archangel and Angel to the Christian and the Musalman, and his existence no more takes from the unity of God in the one case than in the other. It might as well be argued that the Viceroys, the Judges, the Magistrates, the Commissioners, the Generals, the Admirals, of the Empire detract from the supreme authority of the King-Emperor, as that the Devas detract from the supremacy of God. They administer the laws of nature; they help men, women and children, save them from many a danger and encourage them in many a trouble; it is not that they are God — save as we also are God — but that God is in them as in us, and those only can understand the polytheism of Hindus and Buddhists who realize that "for the sake of the Self is the Deva dear". How dreary, how lonely, the world would be, were the only intelligences men and God. How empty it would be, were it not for these Shining Ones who occupy every rung of the ladder above us. There is a vast ladder of consciousness from the mineral to the Lord of the Universe, and we are on one rung of the ladder, differing not in essence from those below us and those above. Devas do not, any more than men, mar the unity of God.

It is true that the Hindu and the Buddhist, like the Greek and the Roman Catholic, take advantage of this *ministry of Angels,* and invoke these divine Ministers. Why not? The Angel, the Deva, incarnates a fragment of the Universal Self, and the light of Brahman shines through him. Is it wrong that the weak tendrils of piety, love and worship in the most ignorant, most foolish, and most undeveloped of the children of the Universal Father, should twine around the radiant form of some benignant Intelligence, more readily to be understood, more easily to be worshipped, than the All-pervading Self? Idolatry? Ah no! not in the evil sense; wrong idolatry is to worship the separated self; right idolatry is to worship the Universal Self in any form that stimulates the intelligence, that quickens the heart.

The worlds of the Hierarchies are the worlds subtler than the physical, incognisable by the physical senses. The Hindu and Zoroastrian books speak largely of these worlds and give many descriptions of them. The Buddha tells us that He has seen these worlds, "the world below, with all its spirits, and the worlds above". Christian and Muslim believe in heaven and hell, and their scriptures tell thereof. It is not worth while to dwell on facts so well known.

4. *The Nature of Man.* Man is divine, a Spirit, in his innermost nature, and wears garments of matter. The Hindu proclaims: "I am He." The Chinese Buddhist speaks of the true man without a position", the jewel Spirit in the lotus of the body. The Fravarshi of the Zoroastrian is the Atma of the Hindu. The Hebrew declares: "Ye are Gods," and the Christian exultantly proclaims that the body is the temple of God. Not so clearly speaks the Muslim, and yet when we find immortality asserted of man, and then read that all will perish save the Face of God [*Al Kuran,* Chap. XXVIII] we are forced to conclude that he also recognizes the identity in nature of God and Man.

And this unity comes out clearly in the Sufi teaching. Jami declares:

> *Thou art absolute Being: all else is but a phantasm,*
> *For in Thy universe all Beings are one.*
> *Thy world-captivating Beauty, in order to display its perfections,*
> *Appears in thousands of mirrors, but it is one.*

In *Gulshan-i-Raz* we read:

> *Thou art the eye of the reflection while He is the light of the eye: . . . when thou lookest well to the root of the matter,*
> *He is the Seer, and the Eye, and the Vision.*

It is sometimes asked: "Has man a Spirit?" No, he has not. He *is* a Spirit and *has* a body. The body does not possess the Spirit, but the Spirit possesses the body. It does not own the Spirit, but the Spirit owns it. The body is transitory, the Spirit is eternal; the body is born into a world and dies out of it, the Spirit is unborn, undying. If you have ever watched a dying man, who knew his own nature, and have seen how the living Spirit rejoiced in the wider, more potent life opening before him as the burden of the flesh was slipping off, you must have realized the truth of the saying that there is no such thing as death, in any real sense. Death is the passing from one room to another, in the house of the universe; death is putting off a heavy coat, and standing in lighter garments. Man loses by death none of his spiritual, intellectual and emotional powers; he loses nothing but the flesh. We are Spirits, Sparks of one Fire, Rays of one Sun; we are in the image of God's eternity; we are enduring as Himself.

5. *His Evolution*. Here a question may burst from the lips of some: "You cannot say that all religions teach the same on this. How can you reconcile the reincarnation of the Hindu with the special creation of each Spirit of the Christian?" Obviously I cannot; the doctrine of a special creation of each Spirit is modern, unphilosophical and blasphemous, and is wholly indefensible. But I may urge that as Christianity did not, till A.D. 533, deny the pre-existence of the Spirit, it is for Christians to explain why they denied the ancient doctrine and forced a heresy on the Christian world. The doctrine of reincarnation — the unfolding by the Spirit of its divine powers through a series of evolving, improving vehicles — is a doctrine common to all ancient Faiths. Hinduism and Buddhism taught it, or, more accurately, founded their teachings on it as a well-established natural fact. The Egyptians based on it their views of the after-death life; Plato, Pythagoras, and the Greek and Roman world asseverated it. The Jews taught it, as may be read in Josephus, the *Kabbala,* and elsewhere. It was the current doctrine in the time of Jesus, and was alluded to by Him on more than one occasion; several Church Fathers taught it; the doctrine persisted in the Christian Church among such sects as the Albigenses; it reappeared strongly in the Church of England, in the seventeenth and eighteenth centuries, and was taught by clergymen of that Church as well as by learned laymen. A little later Wordsworth sang:

> *Our birth is but a sleep and a forgetting.*
> *The soul that rises in us, our life's star,*
> *Hath elsewhere had its setting,*
> *And cometh from afar.*

Once more, in our days, is the doctrine being preached in Christendom by clergymen of the Established Church. There is one sentence, believed by Christians to have been spoken by their Master, which is a far more compelling argument than one which turns on the meaning of disputed texts: "Be ye therefore perfect," He commanded His disciples, "even as your Father which is in heaven in perfect". Perfect as God is perfect. Is it pretended that any one of us, frivolous, foolish, limited, can — before the tomb receives us, or the fire consumes — become perfect as God is perfect, all-knowing, all-powerful, all-holy? What human words may compass a description of the perfections of the Supreme? Yet Jesus did not hesitate to say: "Be ye perfect as your Father in heaven is perfect". How can this command be obeyed, save in many, many lives, in which we shall slowly climb the long ladder of perfection?

Let not the Christian, then, fail to claim his splendid heritage as a son of God: let him claim his birthright to reproduce the divine likeness in himself.

The position of the Muslim with regard to reincarnation is doubtful: some maintain that it can be drawn from *Al Quran*, but it certainly forms no part of the ordinary Muslim religious education. But in the thirteenth century A.D we have the Darvesh Jelal, whose teachings are preserved in the *Mesnavi*, and he says:

> *I died from the mineral, and became a plant.*
> *I died from the plant, and reappeared in an animal.*
> *I died from the animal, and became a man.*
> *Wherefore then should I fear? When did I grow less by dying?*
> *Next time I shall die from the man,*
> *That I may grow the wings of the angel.*
> *From the angel too must I seek advance; all things shall perish save His Face. Once more shall I wing my way above the angels;*
> *I shall become that which entereth not the imagination,*
> *Then let me become naught, naught; for the harp-string crieth unto me; "Verily, unto Him shall we return."*

The position of the Zoroastrian also is doubtful on this point — some Parsis affirm it, some deny it; and we can only point to the fact that Zoroastrianism is "a religion in fragments"; and say that in the Greek and the neo-Platonic writings, which appear to reproduce the Persian teachings, after the destruction of the library of Persepolis by Alexander, the doctrine is taught.

6. *The Great Laws.* By "the great Laws" I mean the Law of Karma, or that of cause and effect; and the Law of Sacrifice, or that of the propagation and the maintenance of life.

The Law of Karma is stated by science in the invariable sequences which it calls laws of nature; the theologian calls it divine justice. It is the rock on which all is built, the true support of all thinking and all activity. It prevails in all worlds, gross and subtle; it is a universal law. It is well stated in a Christian verse: "Be not deceived; God is not mocked; whatsoever a man soweth, that shall he also reap". [Gal, VI 7] Says the Buddha: "If a man speaks or acts with an evil thought, pain follows him, as the wheel follows the foot of the ox that draws the carriage ... If a man speaks or acts with a pure thought, happiness follows him, like a shadow that never leaves him". Hinduism abounds with such passages, and they may be culled from every scripture.

The Law of Sacrifice is the statement of the fact that all lives live by the surrender, forced or voluntary, of other lives; that the outpoured Life of the Supreme is the support of the world. In the lower kingdoms sacrifice is compelled; minerals disintegrate that plants may live, plants that animals and men may live. In the human kingdom, with the great growth of intelligence, the voluntary association of the individual with the universal Will becomes possible. In proportion as that association becomes completer, does spiritual life unfold, and ultimately realize itself. The symbol of the Cross incarnates, for the Christian, the ideal life of sacrifice; and every aspirant for Brahmanhood, for Buddhahood, for Christhood, treads the Way of the Cross.

The student may expand this brief *resume* into a book, and the more he studies the more clearly will shine out the Brotherhood of Religions, as expressed in Common Doctrines.

We have still to consider Common Stories and Common Ethics.

COMMON STORIES

There are certain stories which are told of the Founders of Religions, the outline the same in all; this identity of outline being due to the fact that each Founder is seen as an incarnation of the Logos, and that the symbol of the Logos in all creeds is the Sun.

In very truth the Sun — the source of life and light for the worlds of his system — is seen in the ancient religions as the body of the Logos, His manifested form on the plane of physical matter, while in modern religions the Sun is used as a symbol of the all-pervading Lord, meet image of the One by whom the worlds are supported. The ever-repeated story of the Sun, the annual story for our earth, is the root-truth, the root-mythos, in the physical manifestation of every Founder of a great religion, and Their human lives ever tell again on the world's stage the drama of the Sun.

This statement cannot be made in relation to the religion of Islam, and the reason is obvious. The great Prophet of Arabia is regarded by his followers as purely human, and not as an incarnation of the Logos, and they think rightly; but in all religions whereof the Founder is seen as a divine incarnation, the outline of the great *mythos* appears. The fact has been used as an argument to prove that the Founders had no historical existence, but that is a mistake. The historical life contained the events which reincarnated the *mythos,* and from the historical figure shone out the rays of the divine Sun; it is not that the Sun is the Founder, but that both the Sun and He are physical representatives of the central life of a world-system, and that what the Sun is to his system the Founder is to His religion.

Mithra of Persia had for his sign the Bull, as had Osiris of Egypt, because the Bull was the sign of the Zodiac for the vernal equinox — the Resurrection — when the religion was established; Oannes of Chaldea had the Fish as symbol, for the same reason; Jupiter was Jupiter Ammon; and Jesus was the Lamb, for the same reason.

The Divine Founder is born in a secret place, as Shri Krishna in a dungeon, the Lord Mithra in a cave, the Lord Jesus in a cave — changed into a *stable* in the canonical accounts. The mysteries of Adonis were celebrated earlier, it is said, in that same cave. The birth is at the winter solstice, and is ever accompanied by marvelous events, varying with the nation. Devas rain flowers on Devaki, the mother, and her Divine Son; Angels fill the air with their songs when Mary, the Virgin Mother, gives birth to the Divine Child; divine voices chant that the Lord of the earth is born when Neith, the Immaculate Virgin, brings forth Osiris the Savior; when Zarathustra is born, the light from His body fills the room with radiance; Devas chant joyously when the infant Buddha is born, and in the Chinese writings, though not in the Indian, He is said to have been born of a Virgin mother, Maya, overshadowed by Shing-Shin, the Spirit. The birth of several of these was heralded by the appearance of a star. Krishna and Jesus alike are threatened with slaughter in infancy, the one by Kamsa, the other by Herod. Narada declares the nature of the infant Krishna, Asita speaks of the future glories of the infant Buddha. Simeon welcomes the infant Jesus as the world's salvation. Buddha is tempted by Mara, Jesus by Satan. All these Great Ones heal the sick, cure the deformed, raise the dead.

Thus resembling each other in their lives, the Founders of the World-Faiths are also alike in their deaths. Their death is a violent death, come how it may; and it always springs from the idea of sacrifice, that sacrifice of the Logos by which the worlds were made, enshrined in the Purusha Sukta of the *Rg-Veda*. From that death They rise triumphant, ascending into heaven. Osiris is slain; His body is divided, like that of the Purusha of the Veda; but He rises and reigns. Thammuz is wept over, slain; and rejoiced over, arisen. The story of Adonis is a replica of the Syrian Thammuz. Krishna is pierced by the arrow of a hunter, and ascends into His own world. Mithra is slain; and arises again from the death, the salvation of His people. Jesus is killed; but rises and ascends to heaven. And all the deaths and resurrections fall at the vernal equinox.

These innumerable likenesses cannot grow out of chance; they are the signs of a common story, reappearing continually. The superficial resemblances leap to the eyes as we turn over the pages of the world-scriptures, and the more we study, the more do the common stories reveal themselves, the ever repeated fairy-tales of the World-Legend.

COMMON ETHICS

That sublime morality is a common possession of the World-Religions is a fact too well established to need argument. All that is necessary here is to give a few quotations, enough to indicate the rich veins of metal from which these priceless nuggets are taken.

Returning Good for Evil. Manu says: " By forgiveness of evil the learned are purified"; " Let him not be angry with the angry man; being harshly addressed, let him speak softly". In the Sama-Veda: " Cross the passes difficult to cross; wrath with peace; untruth with truth". The Buddha teaches: "A man who foolishly does me wrong, I will return to him the kindness of my ungrudging love; the more evil comes from him, the more good shall go from me"; "Let a man overcome anger by love; let him overcome evil by good; let him overcome the greedy by liberality, the liar by truth"; "Hatred ceaseth not by hatred at any time; hatred ceaseth by love". Lao-tze says : "The good I would meet with goodness; the not-good I would meet with goodness also. The faithful I would meet with faith; the not-faithful, I would meet with faith also; Virtue is faithful. Recompense evil with kindness". Confucius answered a questioner: "What you do not wish done to yourself, do not do to others; when you are laboring for others, let it be with the same zeal as if it were for yourself." Jesus said: "Love your enemies, bless them that curse you, do good to them that hate you, and pray for them that despitefully use you and persecute you."

Humility and Tenderness. Lao-tze says: "By undivided attention to the passion-nature, and tenderness, it is possible to be a little child. By putting away of impurity from the hidden eye of the heart, it is possible to be without spot. There is a purity and quietude by which we may rule the whole world. To keep tenderness I pronounce strength". "The sage . . . puts himself last, and yet is first; abandons himself, and yet is preserved. Is not this from having no selfishness? Hereby he preserves self-interest intact. He is not self-displaying, and therefore he shines. He is not self-approving, and therefore he is distinguished. He is not self-praising, and therefore he has merit. He is not self-exalting, and therefore he stands high". Jesus teaches: "Except ye become as little children, ye cannot enter the kingdom of heaven"; "He that exalteth himself shall be abased, and he that humbleth himself shall be exalted."

Righteousness more Important than Forms. Manu lays down of action, "mental, verbal or corporeal": "Of that threefold action, be it known in the world that the heart is the instigator"; "To a man contaminated by sensuality, neither the Vedas, nor liberality, nor sacrifices, nor observances, nor austerities, will procure felicity". The Buddha says: "It is the heart of faith accompanying good actions which spreads, as it were, a beneficent shade, from the world of men to the world of angels". Jesus complained: "Ye tithe mint and rue, anise and cumin, and have omitted the weightier matters of the law — justice, mercy and truth."

Thus might I continue to quote text after text on every virtue, and from the tree of every religion similar leaves might be plucked. For all teach the same truths; all are channels of the one life; every scripture repeats the one message, because there is only one great Brotherhood of Teachers, and each who comes forth from it speaks with a single language.

Hence religions are not rivals, and should not be haters of each other. They are children of a common parent, giving out for the benefit of mankind the truths they have learned in the ancestral home. There is a real Brotherhood of Religions, and all who study the religions of the world must recognize the identity of their teachings. To a comparative mythologist all religions are equally false, and are outgrowths of ignorance. To a Theosophist all religions are true, and are the outgrowth of the WISDOM. Each religion has an equal right to every truth, and none may claim aught as his exclusively, "Mine, not thine, nor his". Rather is the true word, "Mine, because thine and his."

There is one Religion — the knowledge of God, and all religions are branches of that stem, the Tree of Life, the roots of which are in heaven while the branches are outspread in the world of men, The heavenly root is the WISDOM — not faith, not belief, not hope, but the knowledge of God which is Eternal Life. From any one of its branches a man may pluck a leaf for the healing of the nations. Let none deny that which to another man is truth, for he may see a truth which others do not see; but let none try to impose his own vision on others, lest he should blind them in forcing them to see what is not in their field of view. There is but one sun, and every energy on our earth is but some form of solar force; as one sun feeds the whole earth, so one Self shines in every heart. There is only one blasphemy — the denial of God in man. There is only one heresy — the heresy of separateness, which says: "I am other than thou, we are not one." We need, for the redemption of the world, more than altruism, noble as that is. We may learn unselfishness, sacrifice, self-surrender, but we do not stand established in the One, until we can say: "There are no others; it is my Self in all." When all man say this, the world will have its Golden Age: when one man says it in life, his presence is a benediction wherever he goes. We are brothers, but more than brothers. Brothers have only a common father; we have a common Self. In all around us, then, let us see the Glory of the Self, and let us remember that to deny the Self in the lowest, is to deny it in ourselves and in God.

www.ingramcontent.com/pod-product-compliance
Lightning Source LLC
LaVergne TN
LVHW041503070426
835507LV00009B/792